Mexico

Gary Allen

AGENDA EDITIONS

© Gary Allen
2013

ISBN 978-1-908527-11-0

First published in 2013 by Agenda Editions,
The Wheelwrights, Fletching Street,
Mayfield, East Sussex TN20 6TL

Design and production by JAC design
Crowborough, East Sussex

Printed and bound in Great Britain
by TJ International Ltd, Padstow, Cornwall

Gary Allen is an award-winning poet from Northern Ireland. He received a major award from the Northern Ireland Arts Council and has been applauded across Ireland for his gritty and honest poetry. He travelled and worked across Europe for many years before settling in Holland for some time, and then returning home.

The author of eleven published collections, from Flambard, Agenda Editions, and Lagan Press, he has been published in many international literary magazines and important anthologies of contemporary Irish poetry throughout Ireland, Britain, mainland Europe, USA, Canada, Australia, and New Zealand, such as *The Threepenny Review, Fiddlehead, Malahat Review, Meanjin*.

His books have been extensively reviewed in major literary magazines and newspapers. Recently a selection of his poetry was published in the anthology, *The New North,* Wake Forest University Press, North Carolina, and in the UK by Salt Publishing.

He has been described as one of the most intriguing and interesting of the younger generation of Ulster poets, and as one of the most distinctive voices of his generation. Gary Allen is also a successful novelist and short story writer.

Acknowledgments

Agenda, Ambit, Antigonish Review (Canada), *Ars Interpre* (Sweden), *Cyphers, The Edinburgh Review, Fiddlehead* (Canada), *London Magazine, The Malahat Review* (Canada), *Poetry Ireland Review, Poetry New Zealand, The SHOp, South Carolina Review* (USA), *Stand, The Yellow Nib.*

CONTENTS

Our cousin sorrow	7
The seventh day	8
The memory pool	9
Outside the city gates	10
A pony and two dogs	11
Lines	12
Just me and the moon	14
Mexico	15
The day John Lennon died	17
The animal house	18
The foundling hospital	19
Keep the faith	20
Garvagh election	22
Sand Sunday	24
A southern sky	26
Crux	27
Walk don't walk	28
Extra-curricular	30
Red	31
Back roads	32
Bevrijdingsdag	33
What is a soul?	35
The falling tower	37
The dead	38
Lily	40
White eyes	42
A rugby match	43
Perpetual motion	45
Checkmate	47
The word returns	48
Flax	49
Goya in Berlin	50
Pie in the sky	51

Chips	52
Kitchen sink	53
Hollywood	54
Wienerwald	55
Elliptical	56
Hundreds and thousands	57
Night trains	63
Nicknames	65
Sixty rounds a minute	66
El Paso	67
Configuration	68
Elephants	70
Points North	71
Frida	73
Kaddish	74
Barranca	75
The boy from tomorrow	76
Next	78
Dénouement	79
The laughing dog	80
Dream as big as Africa	82
The beautiful game	83
Consider my father eating an egg	84
Peasants	85
Shell	87
Nina	89
South of the border	91
Coatlicue	92
Sand coloured cubes	93
Wave	95
Yage	96

Front cover painting:
Diego Rivera's 'Flower Feast of Santa Anita', 1931.
Digital image by kind permission of The Museum of Modern Art, New York/Scala, Florence.

Our cousin sorrow

Baked faces in the sun
all but one knows the meaning of bread

and she is a child of spoil
handing down clothes, even to the boys –
foot-straps, tennis shoes, hockey shirts

a girls' school on a street of plane trees
cardboard art-folders wider than she is
half-a-crown to walk her safely across the morning town.

Steal something for us from your father's shop on wheels
bag of rice, tin of peaches, tomato soup –
yet she is thinner than us
even her gums are bloody.

Let us play a game
a child's game
like dancing around the ancient stones outside the houses
finding a shilling in the sand at Red Bay.

Let us play a game of death
with the wind whipping dust in the broken pavilion
the quick sun scudding shadows across the slopes of Trostan

the old men from the mental hospital
brushing up leaves with brooms
watching us fearfully with giant cow eyes.

The seventh day

The day my lover told me she didn't love me any more
was like cutting pieces from my body:

cutting pieces from your body
can be a kind of love too –

on those wet Sunday afternoons
the light dull with winter
the light thick with soup

my mother would prostrate herself
an angel to a somnolent God

paring his toughened discoloured toenails
slicing the corns with a razor blade
lancing neck boils with hot needles
scraping hair from a languid head

and he let her – love was passive
to his wicked strength

like a spear into the side of flesh
green thorns deep into reasoning
the caresses of a broken body.

How we love our hatred, even in the face
of black storms, mountainous waves

or stones thrown at religion
women and children pushed under the waters of the Bann
the crackle of waste on fire
the smell of another man's love:

the day my love boarded a train for Germany
without turning her eyes in my direction
was a Sunday too, like the clear cut of a drug
the severing of a belief, a Sunday like all the others.

The memory pool

So you come home late and apprehensive
and wonder why everything has suddenly changed
changed, yet subtle as beads of snow
blowing along the dry pavement, like pellets of polystyrene

the night blacker than usual, without boundaries
and the hedges and shrubs stunted
frozen fearfully as a woodland pond

and you wonder, Is this the right house?
the hall stinking like an animal's corpse.

Did I buy these books of poetry
from all the flea-markets and second-hand stalls of Europe?
The scribbled signature on the inside pages looks familiar.

My mind running at a hundred miles per hour –
I first came across you, a filthy child in a coat too large
selling penny sweets from an improvised handcart
queuing patiently among the charred wood and broken steel
for dubious cuts of meat:

I had a doctor friend who drank vodka all night
couldn't sleep for recurring dreams
of maggoty bodies like rubber chickens
bulldozed into pits of lime.

Does all time and memory happen in an hour?
does everything occur at once?

the wind lifting the letterbox
the fire cold, my senses numb
the patterns on the wallpaper running into one another
like the graphs of a diseased brain

and death the planes that carry us back from point to point
in some unknown void –
only the tapping in the flue, Goodbye, Goodbye.

Outside the city gates

In those days the trains ran out to the West as well
single gauge lines
stopping at the shortened platforms of every market town

all the way out to Strabane, down to Garrison and Poyntzpass
dropping off honeymooners at the Loughs or bleak strands
picking up wood, cement, sand, wool, linen, beef

ministers' daughters for the private schools in Belfast
spade-faced farm labourers with sullen families and cardboard
suitcases for the Liverpool mail-boat.

It seems a strange way to strike at an Empire –
the smashed and shattered wood of lone signal-boxes
dynamited water-towers or points:

my father drove a flatbed lorry
down the hilly country roads
following the lines
an iron crowbar on the seat beside him –

a veteran Desert Rat from a real war,
he feared no one
no one else wanted to make repairs

and once outside Coalisland
a single shot cracked the windscreen –
it could have been a stone.

But now the barbarians are among us
the mills are obsolete
the rails have been torn up and sold as scrap

leaving strange elongated grassy embankments
like ancient burial-grounds.

A pony and two dogs

Lazy old fool in your paddock of hardened ground
a wired-off piece of council green

the cowboys are sleeping and dreaming of school
do you see the moon through giant eyelids
a ball of frost above the shadowy outline of the Antrim hills?

The shudder of skeletal flanks
overgrown hoofs rooting in the sparse grass and dung

the ring of lights in the estate
lone cars on the carriageway
single bathroom lamps –

and then two men come into the estate in a white van
set two mastiffs under the wire and into the pen

I hear sounds that are almost human
as I get ready numbly for work

a bone-bag pony skittering into the driveway
eyes wide in terror
two dogs tearing its hide to ribbons

gouging its throat open
ripping off its ears
as they pull it to the ground

and a woman runs out
throws a basin of water over the animals:

the dogs are pulled back into the van
the pony whimpering and dying in pools of its own blood

as I leave wearily for work
a vet is putting it down

and the children gather around –
it is still dark this morning
funny how things happen on the periphery of the mundane.

Lines

Those were the days of long queues
outside the dole offices
cardboard-stuffed shoes letting in rain
the pain of waiting like a sun that never shines
a piece of paper with numbers stamped on it
a piece of paper with your name stamped on it
a cigarette made of tobacco dust
as we did the dole queue shuffle, and waited
without speaking
without hope
without breakfast
and the man at the desk is angry with so much failure
tells us we are to blame
there is plenty of work out there
not the lame schools
or the engrained culture of the loser
or the bleeding state
as we each think like a chain
linked to a string of thoughts
like rain on telegraph-wires
and each of us thinks our own escape
each of us dreams a way out.

Everything is broken
the legs on the table in the kitchen
the rings on the cooker don't work
have burned out long ago
the toilet no longer flushes
bring out buckets of cold water
work a few hours in the slaughter house
for a parcel of cheap cuts
hands slashed like pieces of meat
all the time-insane going round and round
on feet of water in the same direction
keeping stumm with one another
for who knows who will tell
who will succumb to the luxury of deceit.

Cider is cheap, like sex in an empty flat
where hardboard doors have been punched open
whose oil-cloth has been burned for heat
whose rooms echo with desperate voices
the smell of mince and onions in cheap boarding-houses
listen, I will be someone, we will be someone
this one will write a novel
this one will get an interview
she will win the lottery
she will go on the game for a half of whiskey
this one will O.D. in heaven with a smile
these two will find love among the washing-lines
this one will find poems in their dead voices
as the cider runs out
as the queue snakes quietly out of sight.

Just me and the moon

Tie your black hair back with rubber bands
the taut skin goose pimpled
a nude study, a moon frozen in the window

while I break the iced water in the toilet-bowl
warm your clothes at the one-bar electric-fire –

will they need you at the laundry today?
a few hours slaving in the steam
outside, the pavements and streets are covered in slush

and Mrs. Khan pretends
she doesn't understand the wage rates:

you are too sensible in your East European way
to be made a fool of

but what does one do if you want to eat?
look at me –
up to my elbows in rancid meat

in a wooden outhouse near the carriageway
or stretching skin for sausages
twelve hours a day.

How many pairs of underwear, socks, blankets
do you wash and wring and fold?
and Mrs. Khan can't understand a word you say
when you query the money she pushes into your hand.

Yes, things will change, they always do
but not today

like the men who refuse to be served by you
or the meat I steal and trim –
ghosts of our own presence.

Mexico

That was the year of Mexico
tar melted in every street
fires were started along the embankments
of the motorways, cars swerved to avoid stones
and the talk was of Pele

but the shadows were long on the pavements
milk curdled like blood
front doors were propped open by panting dogs
and everything slowed to the sound of the televisions
the far off slam of a train door
of feet running in the next town down the line

like a serial saint who is lost
but is watched as an ant in a glass-case:
my father went to Donegal,
Bury my heart at Wounded Knee
or just South of Buncrana on the Derry road –

he came back late with a blackened eye
and two space guns that shot sparks:
Watch which house they go to –
she poured us lemonade as we watched Germany.
Take care on the way back up the estate,
they'll be waiting with sticks and bottles.

It's the silence you remember, after the cheers
have died away, and the heat trickles like fear
down your spine to the only exit,
and the burned-out shell of a car
the kerbs painted like far mile-stones

as a helicopter settles in the clear sky
and Jesus is beaten for a faith he is not sure of
but becomes a reluctant martyr
in the dust and the broken glass:
who won that year, in the bullring in the sun?

just the same, no one is there at the time of their death
and the evening becomes bruise purple
above the timber-yard
the ragged clouds like flags of smoke
on the far skyline, in another country.

The day John Lennon died

The day John Lennon died
my coffee had grown cold
a film of skin clung to the sides of the chipped mug

and the girl from Platenmakerstraat
had just came by on the street below
forcing her black unisex bicycle over the hump in the road

on her way back from school to help on the sugar beet farm –
she waved, and I thought of her naked
as a radio played pop-music from the other room:

where are you now, my hero?
lost in the lines of a poem about home

and the death of a school-friend in a back alley
who was blown away by a dumdum bullet
for opening tins at an army-base –

these things decide borders.

I had just come back from the Rhine ferry
to clear my thoughts:
that was the time between writing

and cleaning the fluff-balls from behind radiators
in the air-force base outside Arnhem

the bed still unmade
she called from the shower,
John Lennon is dead:

my coffee is cold
the poem will not work
the hero is dead and will not acquiesce

to my martyrdom of him
and I know my girl is a cheat
and I know the hours are ticking down to the evening-shift
after all, this is not a dream.

The animal house

What is it you see behind your eyes?
the world turning round your zenith
just enough to move the dirt in the sink

and the day drags on like half-remembered songs
as you see faces that have long gone
as you walk in places you think you were

across squares wet with grey rain
and parks of closed-over flowers
Sunday swings chained to appease a God

who neither knows nor cares

the mind crowded, yet lucid in self-destructive insanity
from the kitchen to the chair beside the telly
counting cars on the shiny Macadam

in front of the house, going down to a dull coast
what is it you really see?
my lost sister of countries never travelled

my madam Blavatsky
of the dark drawn curtains

the disembodied voice of the telegraph-wires
against the red skies of Sodermalm
of flat Dutch fields and out-of-fashion clogs

the little shop of cardboard-boxes
and a boxer-dog on wheels:

all is well in the void of daytime soaps
teatime news of bombs and quiz-shows
the mishmash of paper-tigers

and lightening trees – it all makes sense,
like the philosophy of Peanuts.

The foundling hospital

Maybe I was an imagined coloured bird
from a far off spice island
a butterfly, a lowly acorn

on a cut-off piece of calico cloth
from a sleeve, or a breast
or a child's christening gown

instead of infested with vermin
so small and still
only bone, a hole in the roof of my mouth

like a moon seen through a thick window
of hard frost
the buttressed walls of two streets meeting

to a close, keeping back the wind:
an accident, a stepping down in luck
to be born instead of carried dead in the womb

measles, malnourishment, whooping cough
take care of this foundling –
she is not a bastard child.

Keep the faith

So what do we talk about now
when love is optional and never talked about?
like the long-dead whispering only in sleep, Touch me

or in daydreams when the sun suddenly leaps
over the park wall and illuminates the tin-bath
hanging on its rusted nail to the kitchen door

or a car-mirror catches the dull brass
of ornamental candlesticks, companion-sets
Moses on Mt. Horeb with his laws

laid down with an iron poker across my back
when I was a child stealing from the drawer
your dead mother on the stairwell, her face mottled

with dust motes, a young stern woman again
with healthy kidneys and unshakable faith –
shall we talk of years narrowing to a tunnel

of glaucoma, the swelling in legs, weeping ulcers
how the heart is in steady decline
how the modern world was once modern to you also?

Keep the faith, my grandfather would say, pulling me
from the water-closet, my small hands pressed
to the linen cloth of the family bible, the blue King James:

let's not talk at all, of blood slowing
in rigid veins, of the dead gurgling in the pipes
like sour water in the intestines

of that other world where the young
were laid out in rows, wrapped like rust red sardines
the great fist of God a hair trigger on a tommy-gun

in the docker bars of Belfast:
listen to the evening fading away down the street
like footsteps, the silence of all the lonely men

guarding dark offices with clicking machines, building-sites
mental-wards, lorries parked up on hard shoulders
dashing into dirty washrooms to jerk off.

Garvagh election

When the evenings clear
everything looks dirty again

like a dead blackbird picked clean
ploughed into the lane
the collapsed tunnels of a strawberry farm

the clumps of moss washed from the slate
by winter's driving rain
into the stone yards

and the sheets hung on wire-lines
in the closes
the sound of a leather ball

beating hypnotically against the gable end
the factory mill-horns
the voices of women at the gates –

even the mountains looked old and used:
then he came
a rally from the past

ghosts raised from bulrushes
the rotting weeds of flax ponds
his voice the hooters of steel ships

tumbling down wooden scaffolding
into oily water –

they put him high on a lorry back
till his head held the sun
till his head blocked every second-storey window

his head a grotesque cartoon on a church ceiling

a large man in a linen hat
a plantation owner

the summer crowd seaweeding him
a band out of tune
to the broad single street of hate.

Sand Sunday

Where were you on Sunday
when God finally gave up in despair?

chained the round-about to a concrete block
the swings together with padlocks

his face became the stone of a statue
on a rain-blurred hill

and all the churches sang in disharmony
like the lovers fumbling in the park shelter
like the old woman keeping warm under newspapers

in the cubicle of the public-toilet.

This is the centre of the earth
all things happen in this corner

the brick of the walls and the back-to-backs
are harder than anywhere
the slate sharper, the voices harsher

the rain more cutting
sin more desperate
hunger more keen

what my prophets have written have become real
here in the faces of these men and women

who love nothing
whose hearts are full of hate –

even the devil would shrivel up and die among them.

I was reading poems from a stolen book
I was between jobs

I was waiting for a blond lover

whose skin was soft
but would keep us apart like thirty years
or the cruel need to be something other.

And God turned away with a shrug
his name washed with too much blood and cordite,
as I transfigured in bitterness.

A southern sky

This uncle went to Australia
the ticket-stubs of a punch-machine
littering the bureau of his King's Cross bedsit –

and nobody saw him
the blue mountains of a dream
the sandy muck thrown up on the racecourse
out at Randwick:

that was in forty-eight
a copperplate name
from a school too poor to be segregated

over the wall from the alabaster statues
the looped-wire crucifixes and the dying flowers.

The best-looking of them all
he couldn't find what he was looking for

in the doorways and ant-infested rooms
of quick sex

the girls stinking hot
like a small constellation

when he stands in the melting park
in the corner of a universe that is not his
the shooting-stars sliding like butter

useless and alone, as an unread letter
as photographs tacked to the wall of a derelict house.

Crux

This morning, they are bringing the body
out of the bottom flat –

what did I know of her?
I heard nothing that was new:

she whimpered all night like a dog –
he had tied her wrists together with tape
super-glued her lips shut

so that she suffocated slowly
faded like the lighted wing of a school-building
in a dull morning.

My grandfather came back from hell
religiously walked the lanes
as the sun came up on the wild woodland flowers

to breathe
rejuvenated
came to an understanding with the dead

that all men must reconcile themselves
to the nature of their coming death
and the endurance of the earth.

I am all alone this morning
only ghosts
in white sterile forensic suits –
how big a small place can become

the slow patter of a light rain
on the tarpaulin in the closed yard

a soft heart-beat that is no more
trussed up and confined in a coal-bunker.

Walk don't walk

All ball-games and cycling prohibited:
look at the sky, an unfathomable blue
an upside down universe, a rabbit-hole
a wind-tunnel, an unmanned border

as you stand at the window, and think,
I have nothing to do today,
pretend to be a part of it.

And is it really true, that there are other cities
just a smoke-trail away?
bringing a different set of genetics
on budget tickets

to work in chicken factories
pick mushrooms
clean our houses
buy expensive cameras

but not mine, I am too poor
a social statistic
a school failure.

Don't walk on the grass,
it's not natural

yet the monk on the bicycle
will deliver a young girl to your door
who has no words
who watches you nervously
who has the vapour tracks of silver planes
on her arms and legs

and I still have a gun with assorted ammunition
that was foisted on me to hide
sitting like a heavy complex in the attic.

My father is angry
is buried beside the railway-line
lies between two assholes who never fought a war
but who were stabbed repeatedly with screwdrivers
stood upright in a ditch:

the people of Auschwitz, Buchenwald, Treblinka
are buried in the sky – ask Celan

the guard in the Kosciol Mariacki tower died halfway
parents weep at John Paul airport –
and I am already a prohibited history,
like a ball, or a bicycle.

Extra-curricular

When I was fourteen I lost my soul
in the great depression of the Seventies
it slipped away in the music-class
like a snow goose in a grey sky

over the frozen playing grounds
and the roofs of the housing-estates

or an orange moon sailing
over the frightened tree-tops
though it was still morning and the stars were out
and the sun sat sullen in the corner of the sky;

or the brains splattered on the school-shelter wall
the fragments of sharp bone embedded in the Tarmac
from the young man who was executed several nights before –

only a few years older than us
he knelt and cried in shocked pain,
and was no more.

My soul has two sides
like a moon
like a dumdum bullet

would not be free
until I let it loose
like the loss of myelin sheaths

like the sparks of an angle-grinder
the white light of an oxyacetylene torch
the stone chips of a headstone

or the laughing feet running in riot
the dust of buildings collapsing into the street
voices too thick to sing, or understand
the metronome in the cupboard.

Red

No one is living
the windows are empty of flame
the earth is a solid sphere of ice

the grass on the council greens razor stiff
and sawdust is barometer heavy
in the doorways of the timber-yard –

that was in seventy-five
the suddenness of a car breaking the corner
made the fine hairs bristle

a badger waiting the sharp end of a spade
a slice of bone moon waiting the dawn

until you reach the lights of the lorry-depot
the clang of tail-gates being shut

and you thought of your brother
sleeping
who is working in Toome

who is being watched from a corner bar
as he carries ladders
tins of industrial paint:

and there it stood
at the traffic-light junction
muscles quivering, tense with fear and strength
hoofs sparking on the hard ground

looking at me, not looking at me
flanks covered in stockyard dung
iron ring in its nose
a string of freezing snot

as it snorted, the white bull
as the lights turned red
as my brother wakened
from a dream of steel travelling into flesh.

Back roads

I know a place that isn't on any map
or measured by a mile stone
or fenced by a triangulation point –

on summer evenings, clouds of black midges play
around the ditch pines
above the stagnant water of the dark bog-land

and it is quiet, as the sun goes down
local people walk other roads
local people are superstitious

believe that those who break the circle
come back when they die
to answer for what they have done

and there are things to find
if you dig into the moss bank
a twisted piece of steel comb

a fragment of bone too small
to be swept into a plastic-bag
shoe leather, button, bent coin, the torn heart

of a playing-card that has survived
the fire heat, the petrol heat, the sunlight
wind, rain, hail

and the locals say, You notice
how the bridge hill dips
has settled to a permanent crater?

Pine-cones fall like thunder-claps
to bounce across the road
telegraph-poles lean together from the soft earth

carrying electric whispers on the charged air –
local people say, when the breeze is right
you can hear a work-van approaching.

Bevrijdingsdag

I saw a girl drown
no one seemed concerned
just another junkie from the park
just another roll and coffee and doorway

existence no longer real
she flung herself from a novel
she flung herself from the highest parapet

of a city bridge
while students cycled out of life
concerned with world events and India

thirteen civilian faces on blocks
in front of the HEMA building
photographic exhibition from my past

like the holocaust photographs in the town-hall
like the photograph in De Telegraaf

none of the men who fucked her
knew her broken face
the junkies who shared needles
never knew she was there:

the rows of low houses on the other side of the line
are squatted in now
the process-cheese factory is a square windowless tin:

in this city, I wrote my first novel
that sunk like blond hair beneath dirty water
or frayed curds in great vats
combed and raked and nauseating

that other girl sleeps uneasily in our rooms
the lights on like a train through a dull morning
the pages of my novel floating face-up in the toilet –

such is martyrdom, my love
such is liberation, my love
such is shared pain.

What is a soul?

I'm going East again:
I've just heard the news
like brain-static on a close evening

like heavy chintz curtains,
a mobile on the bedside cabinet
waiting to ring –

a girl I know has just died
the words cold with meaning
the words careering down like sudden rain

warm as wind –
she is dead
she has killed herself

without a thought:

someone has phoned me with the news
I don't know him
his voice is distance

hard as a cooling-board
steel-sharp as a cutthroat
as the word funeral

a time in the near future
a day without weather
his relationship to everything.

What is the soul?
a kinetic dog's head on an Amsterdam windowsill
a pedal-bin of used condoms and tissues

the rind of cheese on the wash-rack
minute fragments of dried blood on a porcelain bath

no, the soul is the silence of everything
that can jerk you into the future
a metaphysical inertia

the black and white of what is
and is no longer there –
like being left behind on a revolving planet.

The falling tower

When you pile-drive the piles through the soft sand
you reach the firm stuff on which the stanchions of iron
and concrete will stand, the ghostly tunnels, the canyon
halls, from the Oud Zuid to the Noord, under all this city,
the Markermeer, the gabled houses, the soft muck of a
fishing village at a swamp's mouth. This unseen mechanical
worm spins its tail south, flinging back soil and gravel,
spitting out fish bones, pottery, sacrifices that have sunk
like tiny unimportant apologies for those who were there
and are gone – like tourists. This is the hum of machines
below the city, the pulse of girls on the Warmoesstraat,
rotating fans, spice and grain ships on the Damrak,
and here I sit, hands, face, boots covered in thick clay,
the overhead garbled string of lights turning the eerie gloom
to day, eating bread and wondering about all this,
what it takes to earn enough to make desolation pay:
if my world comes tumbling down, trapping me
in a pocket of stale air, my muscles will waste, the skin
sag, cankers and open sores will cover my body,
before I am found. In the Begijnhof the single and widowed
women are pious, and pray, give succour and healing
to the sick and lost, the fallen – she is reading Giovanni's Room
above me, but I have no home, no history, no future,
water trickling from the walls, light bulbs dimming
in the safety vents, as houses sink and tumble from the sky.

The dead

My mother said she would never beat me
before I went to bed
no matter how much I asked for it

afraid that in the morning
she would find me dead –

I suppose it doesn't matter now
that we are both nearer death

and every morning hour like a long dead star
brings loneliness instead.

Am I dead yet?
my brother would ask
his eyes closed against the streetlight

the car-lights on the cracked ceiling,
Yes, I said, and no one cares
or cries for you,

like the crying in the room below
the covered plate of stale bread
the cold fatty bacon.

What will you be when you grow up?
Dead – a pair of Wellingtons and a flat cap
that never came home.

Your bandages are too tight
let me cut them
the pus oozing out, on to my fingers

a skin on your cold tea
as you hold back the pain of my touch
stare at the sunlight in the window –

what do you see mother, now that your eyes are stone?
everything as it was before
the long and empty passageways of the soul.

Lily

Our lady of the condom packet
missionary dreams in the Philippines
the sly fag, the curling-tongs like dead lilies

listless as a wet Sunday afternoon
on the entrance table of the Mount Morris Tabernacle,

pray for our sister who is gone
like a crow's wing in a muddy lane
bales of hay rotting in a draughty barn

the paintings and photographs of church Elders
hanging on the wooden walls
of this Gospel Hall in the country

for who else among the people
in their grim blackness
will pray for her?

the wayward child who was too young
and gay as Spring
fresh as sea water in a seaside pool

the monotonous chanting
like the spluttering of a rusty motorcycle
in the muck of a farmyard

through the flapping bed sheets on the wire-line:
she wanted more
than the thin pages of a King James's bible

of river water on a white surplice
the hours of youth draining
through the net curtains of a high bedroom.

Our lady of the lost buttons
and the lace doilies
for the church fair

prayer like a small calibre shotgun
in a girl's mouth on a Sunday afternoon

too weak to break the bone of the skull
leaving only a curious bulge.

White eyes

Who are these sharecroppers
all done up in their best gear
no oil-stains or farm muck
on their bibs and tuckers, church-going bonnets?

fathers, children, grandmothers
lined three deep along the spans
of this iron railway-bridge
smiling, half-smiling, shying away from the sun

in a sort of triumph:
the picture so sharp you could count each rivet
but who would want to record this anyway?
a box-camera fixed on a sand bank or levee

on the slow flowing river shaded with cottonwoods –
and then you notice the two black bodies
swinging from thick ropes, still as reflections,
she looks so peaceful now, at ease

in her best Sunday dress, eyes open
the knotted noose pulling her head to an angle
bare feet a lighter shade above the muddy water
of this baptismal river

dignified, beautiful – who cares or remembers her small sin?
they are singing for you sister
in the wooden Baptist Churches of the Delta –
and then you feel ashamed

at the names of these unimportant backwaters
Derry, Belfast, Allentown.

A rugby match

The December fields of Down
bare as the winter paddy fields of Japan
a landscape without a field:

a poem without a tree is not a poem –
George Moore said that, about a novel

or a thought
someone's hand reaching out of the screaming past
who calls himself my father

though he is only bone now
laid to rest like every stony field
that is turned over.

At Ballynahinch they fight with balls
on dull Saturdays –
no one watches, a funeral line

the sound of muck sucked through boots
my father betting his life on a racing-page
his blood dried and rotten and gone
into dark soil:

look at the farmer
a tight-assed, tight-lipped sort
who would run his stock into the ground

to save a pound on feed
striding along the cracked furrows
three fields in from the roadway

do you suppose he sees or hears or cares
what might come up with the seasons

how tubers split and grow in the wind and rain
the feral sunshine?
like pebbles rattling at Kilroot

mud-caked, clay splattered
his own stink warm in his nostrils
impervious to shouts or claps or death.

Perpetual motion

How did we get here, to this point in time?
having crossed from one parallel line to another
footprints big as basalt columns
yet small as a cancer cell:

All is well, the children shout
voices sure as adults
voices unsure as adults

my mother finds bus-money beneath settee cushions
my father cries, I am dying,
as we turn him over.

Listen to the man on the radio
he is as vaguely familiar
as yellow rent books, old coins

doorways to factories, work-shops, depots
yet he can't be the same man
who told in monotonous black and white

of van-bombs and nuclear reactors
and assassinations and civil rights

of churches burning, bodies swinging, skin blistering:
and my mother ties old clothes in a sack
scrapes butter from a flattened packet
thin as Chamberlain's voice on a Sunday

many years ago
long before you sprang awake in a block of flats
east of Europe

bread hard as iron
hard as heavy water.

The schools are gone
De Lorean is gone –
my mother always thought he was too smooth
the shipyards silent as a pick axed wall

and yet we are still here
breathing as open-mouthed fish in a dynamited pond
nothing in common with the atoms we started with.

Checkmate

Consider the old sodium streetlights
concrete heads stooped over at street-ends
orange hue just as the sun sets
behind the mills, the shipyards, the waste-grounds

the rings of the gas-works
the walkways of bridges opening into no-man's land
spanning dark water and stinking mudflats

as bats zigzag from the top windows
of the boarded terraces, row upon row
a giant chessboard without pieces

everything waxen under their spot-light
throwing shadows across the street to run through
the warren of familiar side-streets and dead-ends
that you keep to like a rat along the wall

the pump that makes the small hairs on your neck
bristle with electricity
that gushes blood into your throat

as a car crunches slowly over glass
freewheels into the next street

you count house-numbers till it stops
listen intently for an engine revving
a moustached idiot in a leather jacket

sandbags and wire-mesh round a shebeen
a pool-table and crates of stolen beer
rigged-up overhead lights

bright and sharp as a butcher's knives
as the Beatles sing, Let it be
and the jukebox is turned up full-blast.

The word returns

An American Pastor came to our Gospel Hall on Sunday
from the cottonwoods of Mississippi
to the motorways and slaughterhouses of the Braid.

He spoke the same as us, but different
and his suit was shiny, well-made
his passion wild as an old-time preacher

in the bog-meadows or the flax-fields
and the distance travelled between each of us was smaller
than an unborn child's sin

or a young girl's lust in a moment of boredom
a Roman hand on the scripture's page
a crucifix at the teacher's table.

And he was able in his tongues of fire
to see the devil's work in many places
from the highest in corrupt power

to the disobedient wife, the doubter
the forces that nailed Jesus to the wooden cross
the twisted lies of Babel.

Friends, he shouted, Christian neighbours
repent before the word of God
for stone upon stone will weigh you down

and crush the breath and bone from your body:
as the hall shook with Hallelujah and Amen
as the clapboard walls vibrated with site-traffic

clearing land for new housing
as feet stamped the wooden boards
like the 1859 Revival of Reverend S.J. Jones.

Flax

Jesus said let the brown flax rot for three days
in stinking pools
before it can be bleached white again

sweating, a human corpse sweating its way to heaven
crude nails tearing the flesh on a cross of wood

and man is only suffering after all
a bag of bone and shit

as my father shouted Jesus
every time he hit us with a sewer rod

as the women gathered at the well for water
in the green bulrushes
as the women weighed the flax with stone

my mother cut open sacks of old clothes
sent by the church
covered over the holes.

My father sits in a wooden watchtower
above the bleaching greens
an angry God confused in poverty

as the body of Jesus is broken
under the thuds of the beetling boards
the blood and waste oozing from his linen shroud

and after three days he stands again and says,
Let all those who love me understand,
Let all my sisters love me like a man.

Goya in Berlin

The Spanish girls are cheap
they make them walk like that
look, I put a needle in my arm:

Jesus was Spanish
Goya painted him like that –

did Goya scrape squashed insects and muck
from the car windscreens
at the roadside?

I have a Turkish friend who listens to me
at night we smoke hash and count the stars
fill in forms we never return.

Sometimes it's just easier to meet men in the trees
dogs are tied to shrub ends
as we do it
standing in dog piss and used condoms.

Madrid, Madrid – I saw that in the window
of a travel agent's
queues outside the cinema
like a line of men with bare chests.

And all the men look the same
on the subway trains –
does God ever see what he creates
did Jesus really die for each of us?

Sometimes, I see a sparkling ocean
imagine that all of us are a mass of silver sardines
in the bottom of a fisherman's boat

living flesh, writhing and reeling
about and under and through each other
like maggots gleaning the last morsel of meat from an ass's jawbone.

Pie in the sky

The men are hanging round the petrol-station
though it is closed
the rusted chain loosely looped

the BP sign turned round
the tyre and engine-oil signs flaking from the brick wall
beer-caps studding the soft Tarmac of the forecourt

caught in the last slants of the sun
they have nothing to do
they have no priest or minister to speak for them.

My father applied for every penny job
until the soles of his shoes wore thin as religion –

that was back in the late Forties
when everyone was still war hungry
and he felt he was owed something for the sand in his lungs

but bigotry endures when borders are gone
buildings rebuilt
and his parents' minister said,

There is no work
and charity without work is a sin
a waste of man's esteem:

the men are like ruffled pigeons settling for the night
along the stone ledge of the petrol-pumps
they want to burn everything down –

the garage doors are closed and seep oil
the plywood box-office is empty
a phone rings then suddenly stops

as the sun sets behind the North facing saw-edged roof
of the engineering-works
the solicitor's office, the gargantuan bank
and my father turns the telly on and sleeps.

Chips

We were so hungry
we could have eaten our way through the Book of Kells
and all the false Saints

yet God did not manifest himself to us
in illuminated gold block letters

but in the sixpenny grease-proof chip bags
whose insides we sucked dry of vinegar and salt.

The unemployed men like bent H's
leaning against the walls of the public-bars

delicate storks, they stood on one foot
to hide the holes in their socks
the thin soles that walked the roads looking for work

or picking berries from the hedges
lifting nearly a whole field of potatoes –

Give us a chip, son, they'd laugh,
Stout fellows, my mother called them
until there was no work in our house

and the days turned slowly with the hours
and the men like monks hung in their own hands
out on the steps, counting the cars going somewhere else.

At least you have the right faith,
the soapbox boys told them,
If you want to throw a stone at something, try the chapel.

and the flax rotted under its own worthless weight
and the shipyards stunk with oily water
and at night we listened to our stomachs dreaming of chips.

Kitchen sink

The sixties are remembered in black and white
old movies and giant gongs
big square sinks for washing clothes, and kids

homelessness, slums
lost reporters in rubble streets
after the action has moved on

from the one good channel that still worked
with a hard slap, a sharp kick.

War men with sticking out ears, bad teeth, frayed scarves
killed along the border
empty-eyed from driving-licence photos.

A running boy, familiar thin and bony faced
a bicycle factory, a sailor falling downstairs
a toy car in the gutter

and children burned to death in a caravan
a hop-picker washing from a bucket, waist down.

Pull the curtains apart, my father spoke
a disembodied voice from the twenties
like a gun-shot in the weeping gloom,

She is dead and buried now –
the two-thirty at Newmarket had still to be run

and everything that was then, was over,
or just begun
like the luminous orange faces on the first colour television
like the light flooding in.

Hollywood

My father looks like Jean Genet –
priest, boxer, orphan runaway
stealing pounds from his wife's purse
small amounts from his children's school savings accounts

paving-slabs and cement in the back of his lorry
ruined stock from cleared-out shops.

My father looks like a Kray
government-marked from his driving-licence photo
hair oiled with butter and receding
thick woollen scarf knotted under his chin
a guillotined head open-eyed upon a cooling board

or Cary Grant in a black beret
outside an Alexandria casino
a Sten gun slung around his shoulder.

Mr. Woodbine, romantic face in a photograph
slack jawed with all his teeth removed
Hollywood pyorrhoea with a blackened eye.

An old matinée movie
a lights-on bone house moving out like a blazing room
in a grey morning above the housing estate.

The day he died, naked in a mixed ward
a silver cigarette-case snapped closed
a cowboy punch to a square jaw
the thick desert in his throat rattling, the last round-up.

Wienerwald

Sharon's hair is black like oil
Sharon's hair is black like soot
Sharon's hair is dry like ashes:

I met her in a Nazi poster
I met her running through the Prater like a giant Ferris wheel
the Turkish men waiting patiently in the earthen hollows

I met her on my tongue.

Come to my aunt's house
a black dress hangs in the wardrobe
wood shavings cover the floor
shaved hair fills the mattress

this large wooden radio jigs
waltzes like nails hammered into wood
chicken livers stink in bowls
the butter melts like bones.

Sharon waits for me on a bridge to Bratislava
Sharon turns to stone in Limerick
Sharon is stomach pumped in a Viennese hospital

while I watch snuff movies from Mexico
dream of escaping to South America
think of the knitted llamas on my aunt's dressing-table.

These old secret black and white films
keep coming to the surface –

naked girls made to run in a forest clearing
Sharon's perfect body
on top of a pile of corpses in a lime pit.

Elliptical

My mother looks into drawers, down cushion seats
for things that had happened, or might happen in the future

black Victorian pennies, silver tanners
a promise from Donegal

a broken photograph
from a war in England –

she knows things that remain unspoken
how everyone made decisions that led them to this place
how life slipped away, like detergent bubbles down a sink

that love happened only in books
that existence was mundane
that children asked for the moon

diazepam nullified the clear moments into dull apathy
a second more of a hand pressing on a child's face

would end everything, but she sensed the peace it would bring
the stillness within a day without hours.

Hundreds and thousands

i

This is the end of a continent
places we don't know how we have come to

or why

the metaphysical
the natural impulse that leads us here:

sand flats and marram grass
the salty pools of sea water

and the planes coming in to land
silver envelopes out of the dark clouds.

Bundled out of the car
far from the city

the ground sucking at your high heels
as you make for the light of the only farm house

the sausage eater will give you a lift back
and takes you quickly against the ditch

as his wife brings in the washing
as you stare at your muck covered shoes.

ii

He is always walking out
the Burberry coat between the hall and the front door
always between a wooden horse and Troy

the briefcase heavy with work and hours.

The child's eyes are big
burnt toast thick with butter

and sprinkled with tiny beads of coloured sugar.

Her mother sits upon the bed
fixing her stockings to clips

with tight rolled balls of newspaper
lightening bruises with powder

while she phones.

iii

The girl is skipping up the concrete stairs
her mother is naked outside the flat

on the floor below

she helps her up
and gently leads her back to their rooms –

she is embarrassed by the thick tangle of pubic hair
her mother's calloused feet –

why do men hunt?
how do they know which women to pursue?

once a man in a comical beret
followed them from the supermarket

for several blocks, in pouring rain

and although her mother hurried them along
she kept looking back to see that he was still following.

iv

All around is hard breathing
echoes in the semi-dark of the boiler house

she removes her underwear
feels them touch her roughly –

she feels like a piece of well-fingered meat

they stand close
yet seem unsure what to do next

panting mouths, lifeless bone:

on the way home from school
the girls in her class gather on the iron railway bridge

the sharp stones ring clear
on the metal meshed walkway

as though ashamed, they shout slut.

v

Father's fingers are fat
his hands and arms are dark with hair

he moves through each room
as if he were counting the years

proclaiming that he was never really there
when her mother discovered the world

was honed to sharpness
the razor edge of words and quietness

the faces of men seen through hangovers
are always the man she married

and now can't remember
but feels under her fingertips

in the flat fields of the bed.

vi

It is the emptiness that slowly fills the heart
when even the familiar is preferable to being apart

and the bead curtains swing apart
and the tired woman falls apart
and the sad sex is painful in the rented room

where nothing is her own
where everything is second hand
where mouths taste of ashes

and you wonder why
and you wonder what you are doing here
and you sometimes think you had a child

and it seems predestined
as a salmon springs up the river
as an eel finds the sea

as a man will always crave flesh

that the child will find you
that the child will despise you
that the child has learnt from you

what she will always hate and desire.

vii

And who by fire?

this little balloon has taken five years
to swell and explode –

the child finds you on the floor
your head has broken fragments from the wooden table

your skin is blackened
fingertips leave indentations in the body
saturated, gorged with its own blood

footprints filling up with water

or like those boot prints in the freshly fallen snow
you follow to places you have never been before

along the tram tracks
to the warehouses of the shunting yards
where the women smoke and open up to foreign workers

hungry like sex, the slushy traces
that suddenly vanish across the frozen waste.

viii

Can you smell the sea
or only the oil and leather and cigarettes
of the sausage eater's car?

He never speaks
he is the brilliant lights on the motorway

the blues and reds and yellows
of the service station forecourts

and all the thoughts that come to you
in such a small confined place

in such a little span of time

is everything out there in the void
of space and stars and sand flats

is everything in the void within

the medulla uncurling at high speed
the blood punching through the artery walls

the lights on the sandy forest path
the intimate smell and decay of the soul.

Night trains

Even in the night –
the collective sleep of fear

that we will not wake –

mail trains cross the vast expanse
of our minds

the sudden light in a water closet along the line
the flickering dynamo down the cinder track.

The corn fields are waiting
the fire towers in the forests are waiting
the irrigation pumps in the ditches are waiting

to open, like the sun

the subconscious talk we never remember
as we wait to open,

like the sun

like the first walk back from her house –
the freight trains shunting blindly in the yards –

nothing sleeps, everything is heroin clear

hundreds of moths dying against the light,
oxyacetylene sparks.

Let us hug the wild coastlines of our pillows
beneath the ruined Norman castles
or dart out across the great boglands

where millions of years are buried

all the dead
holding together the nightmares of their broken skulls

not even the confines of churchyard walls
or words spoken on Sundays

and the alarms nudging nearer,
the great and good in this country of lies
coming to the shock-end of deep tunnels.

Nicknames

Horse is dead
breast bone a giant clamp

he died, though they took the country out of him
with a needle

into the ground with a thump
good black soil for seedlings

on rainy days
the clay will mould you to the worm –

that was my name –

with the sun and neglect
the hogweed will grow through anything

even metal, even bone

the rusted husk of a Ford
on waste ground outside the village

stripped of anything that was good
leaving cider bottles, scattered hemp seed

torn pictures of naked women
exercise-books of algebra

one an impossible dream
the other Orion's Belt –

we were more than the sum of names.

Good teeth you had
the jaw bone of an ass

the best way to London is to keep on running
like the hot iron in your father's forge

liquid metal in a cast.

Sixty rounds a minute

Cramped for hours on the cold floor
watching the border roads
through the scummy jagged glass of this old camper-van

upended in a scrap-yard of wrecked cars
the chassis of tractors and trailers
the rain washing sewage from the busted tankers

high-velocity punctures:

an old man, simple minded
eats broth at the kitchen window
they ripped the heads off every one of his chickens
left them outside his front half-door

as I watch a cat creep from the sandbanks
a young rabbit screaming and struggling in its steel jaws
sliding under the rust-riddled body of a humped-backed caravan:

death is never instant
life never lets us go easily –
I guess someone must have told
I guess someone is always watching.

For an hour I listened
to its high-pitched squeals wishing it would die
a child in frightened pain

its leg-spasms beating a tattoo
against the underside of the caravan
or on a paint-tin lid in the thick of nettles
until, thank God, there was silence.

El Paso

Mexico is a fun place
carnivals and skulls, Popocatepetl and Ixtaccihuatl,
a lost summer's day.

Me and my friend read Kerouac
in a stone quarry
two grey ghosts dropping sticks of dynamite into holes
and running like hell

slabs of mountainside slipping down
as if sliced by cheese-wire.

The work-hut was our Hudson scow
in a sea of rock
our cinema/bordello.

I wanted to go to Amsterdam that summer
he wanted to cross a border
follow the silver trail out of El Paso
mules and cacti and mirages of mica.

We read Fante and Trocchi and Lowry
lying in the rubble, covered by mountain weed
sweating the highland sun

as we waited the lorries coming back to the depot
from the crushing-plants, the road works
to vault the tailgates that would take us back down again.

He wanted to get out
but was found in the side street of a seaside resort
in a builder's skip

his face stabbed so many times with a broken umbrella
by two lads who thought he was queer
faggot books in his work-coat pockets,
he was unrecognisable –
me, I just wanted to get away that summer.

Configuration

The good people are bringing their meals
onto the barges
the good people have finished their honest work
the Romany children are throwing their dogs into the water.

It is a fine summer evening
people are drinking wine on the doorsteps
and laughter carries a long way

settles on the fire-red windows of the hospital
the air-condition units
the iron bedsteads
the bucket trolleys of grey limbs and body pieces
the furnace chimneys.

Lovers have taken their love outside
to the green parks
the rooftops
the subways –
children are too idle for homework or sleep or anarchy.

The mental patients try to sit at peace on the benches
in the asylum grounds
no one screams in anger
no one hammers brains to death
the nurses make silly hats out of the morning's newspapers
like sailing-ships on a calm pond.

It has all become one
with the endless stretching sky
the lazy sirens
the flaking paint on the window-ledge
the cool jazz

a crisp girl sitting naked in the mirror –
she must be my lover, I think –
the long reams of written words
on the paper before me
that will end inevitably in failure
that will end like everything
like every evening
like every feeling
in death and movement.

Elephants

Last night my mother died:
I was writing a poem about death
when suddenly death became real

as a car-bomb under the writing-table
as a radio-station hissing static
and setting your teeth on edge
or the line at the open window
between light and darkness.

And what would it mean now?
the words on the page
the handwriting that was always mine
in the list of things that would have to be done
that were no longer abstract

of the people one is forced to see again
the alien handshake
the young minister who has never met me
or will again

the inanimate flowers that are dead as stone
cold as skin
dry as atrophied blood
listless as snow.

My own condition will always be paramount:
I was writing a poem that needed to be said
that demanded finish
to be as exact as any completed life
to be as empty as a night without sleep
to be a lighted room dulling into morning.

Points North

Here is a life that is dead
it has moved from rest to decay:

that fat side of beef on the hospital bed
waiting for visitors
waiting for medicine
waiting for his bowels to move

is as life-inspiring as a sea slug –
there is nothing there
behind the eyes,
he is only a pair of sucking lips

there is nothing there
like the imbecile trying the door at the end of the ward
led away, his legs take him back again
a mechanical monkey on a bicycle

like the woman who can't sit upright
has fallen across the bed
her hair dragging the floor, and crying for help

like the dried-up potatoes on the plate
the young nurses wet as a Saturday night
the different forms and names for death.

The moment is never exact
the last breath waiting in the lungs
the bile oozing from the mouth
the impatience of those waiting round the living corpse.

Death, like a polished wooden hand
a cow's picked jaw-bone on a stony beach
sand flies on bladderwrack and rotting fish
the arterial blood from a bullet wound to the temple
from a small pistol in Vietnam

is nothing much, just old washing on a line
the yellow pages of a paperback book
the plastic apparatus of a hospital
a new nightdress, and a pair of white shoulders

that still look young
freckled from the sun and coded with the DNA
of a wall-chart on some office wall.

Frida

The day Frida Kahlo was carried on her bed
through the market streets of coloured calico
broken-backed like a giant captive carrion bird

I was sinking under, an ice-pick in the back of my head
a pair of huaraches on a poor waitress's feet
a lover in a cupboard of stale worn-out clothes –

they thought I would die too
ruptured poems in red spined exercise-books
penny-journals of Kit Carson, and heated Irn-Bru

in a ward of adults ashamed of their nakedness
too big to complain, cryptic talk like the sea
gushing down channels in my ears

lying flat under a mirror of small words:
the day Frida Kahlo became a black skull
a crazy lover in a mural
a crazy set of brightly coloured prints in a waiting-room magazine

that looked crazy and out of kilter to me,
I found the immensity of art in myself
in the mending of a broken body
in the defiant eye of a self-portrait with a big hair-do.

Kaddish

My mother has a conversation with God
when she is hanging out washing on an ice-cold afternoon
ash from the dust-bins cutting into her eyes –

he listens
he doesn't answer
he doesn't hold the wooden pegs
a good husband

she sings with him when he is on Sunday television
she knows all the old hymns
she knows how to suffer

like a cattle-truck
like a finger across a throat.

He was there when her mother died
when her father called his name three times
into a whitewashed room no bigger than a coffin.

He turned her onto her side when she shook violently
and bit her own tongue
when she went off into space and returned

vomiting into a bowl he held:
when she died, thirteen faces stood around her bed
weary angels waiting for the right moment

to flip the switch on the gurgling ventilator –
God said nothing
how could he?

My mother died with her God
I live fearful with mine:
if no one is left to worship him

sing his praise,
does God still exist?

Barranca

I am sorry you are not a mechanic
toe-rag boy

(just like us
but not as poor
not as black)

or perhaps you were –
in reverse

mercury-tilt switch, soldered pipes
electric-shocks to genitals, crude waterboarding,
perhaps you could become el Presidente?

We all start somewhere
we all become oxymoron in our beliefs:

we had our place deep in the woods
the leaves falling in the late sunshine
a rope-swing over a natural ravine of bog

where people dumped old prams
shopping-trolleys
dead decomposing dogs

here we would meet to cut-up frogs and mice
fledgling birds

and once we tossed an English boy
over the side
into the bottomless slime –

but we grow-up
drift away
the ravine deep only in our past minds:

my friend joined the navy
and when he came back he became a murderer
justifying everything – just like you, el Presidente.

The boy from tomorrow

I have two cancers –
one eats my blood
one eats my skin

do they know each other?
what do they know of their host?

When I was a child I wanted to kill myself
but I wasn't sure how it was done

the many ways a body may break
or pour forth what is life

to become nothing,
yet the hours were endless
the words in the school-books without meaning

the long dark days without meaning
the rain on the Tarmac yard
the wet pigeons on the potting-sheds
the girls from another planet

whose bodies and bare legs and skirt-tails
were farther than the moon
than understanding

but who went with other boys
into the cross-country copse
and pulled them off in their trousers.

The pine trees thick and dripping
by the barracks watchtower
the mould on the clay pots and dried-up husks of insects

spoke of things dead, like the dying sparks
in the metal-workshop.

Now I knew death again
bodies that have stood outside department-stores one moment
and then were gone

friends who had gone out for a pint
and were left in alleys with throats cut
heads pounded open with pickaxe handles

I have listened to breath stop
have watched the human become inhuman

the people I have loved shed their skins
weary of life
their brains shut down like computer screens.

My cancers take hold, inside and out
without any input from me
cells that know with certainty
how to commit suicide without emotion
how to nail limbs to a genetic cross.

Next

When my father beat us, it was always with humour,
Next please! like in a barber's shop,
Next please!

Next please! I slapped a Dutch girl
on the train up from Dublin
watched by a priest and two old women

all because she wanted to change sleeping positions
for the third time –
Next please! we never spoke again.

I learned quickly how to hit out,
it took a long time to un-learn.

And one Saturday night, coming back from the pub
he fell through the door as we were watching
The Billy Cotton Show, Dixon of Dock Green
on the one good channel of the analogue television

his face like a butcher's block –
I felt like laughing – Fuck you!

We were always close, he told me
as he ebbed in and out of consciousness –

Yes, I thought, at an arm's length
at a foot's distance, the last on the line
of a toy train, Black and White minstrels.

Dénouement

The first short story I published
bought me a cheap blue suit
for my aunt's funeral:

there would be many more, funerals and cheap suits
cloth that came apart at the seams
coffin-lids that were kept closed
to hide the agony of disfigured faces,

Unnatural deaths, they whispered,
The wrong place at the wrong time,
No smoke without fire –

the dead cannot put the record right,
like a crafted story with a subtle end
or a bespoke suit made with love.

My aunt went out like a light-switch
flopped back on the bed
eyes turned-up white, mouth opened in shock
a shopping-list for her daughter twisted in her hand –

what a story her life would make
all the human dramas, perhaps too much
for us to understand, the mundane line between two points

like the humiliation of my father's corpse
naked on the bed of a mixed ward

my cousin's comic head
three times its natural size, without teeth or jaws
the wounds stitched-up like the pattern for a bad suit,
or a crap story without a spell-binding dénouement.

The laughing dog

The thing about death is, you need to know when to let go:
bloody in a council flat, they didn't think I would live
bloody in the old railway-yard
the sound of hurley sticks snapping bone

you stop struggling, want to drift away
but the cold brings you back to earth with a jolt.

The Sunday-school teacher made us eat words from the bible
the minister with the plumb mouth
kept our stink at a distance

the penny-pinching shopkeeper
would wait until the shop was full of Mass-goers
to refuse us tick – you stand dirty in the corner and die.

The thing about death is not its end
but how to leave –
I count the times I have died

scars on a bare-knuckle fighter's face –
the morning I was shot sitting in a builder's van
listening to Them and Van Morrison

the foreman, a part-time soldier
staggered across the road, and dropped
his mouth open on ill-fitting dentures
his bib secured with wire
and the funny missing part of his head –

or stabbed in the neck by a junkie in Amsterdam,
she thought I was her father:
I keep faith, and now I am older

I wait, for all the times I should have died
to become the one full moment
the cancer that is slow to rise

like the hospital helicopter from its landing-pad beside the lough:
and I want to walk into a desert with a little dog
I want to speed-dose in LA, into the palm trees
I want to die far from the reality of my body.

Dream as big as Africa

My mother can't walk any more
she wants to give up
her legs are swollen like an old cow elephant's
with age and heat and dehydration.

When I adjust the tight bandages
the yellow pus runs through my fingers
from the ulcers

she wants to cry out
she wants to let the dry dust blow over her
she wants the sky above her to fill with cold stars:

I awake in a room that is not the room
I was born in
or locked in to be quiet –
my legs are fine for the moment

in the cool evening cackling hyenas
rip and twist and tear
the soft meat from her womb

vultures pick at the eyes and bones
in my dream she asks for water
a heel-print of muddy water

in my dream I am useless
as an unmarried man
as a man without off-spring.

My mother's legs each weigh a ton
her eyes are wet
yet we both laugh at my carelessness.

In this room I am beginning to see the dark
in this darkness I hear her walk again
like teaching seven children to walk for the first time
she is bumping into chairs and bookshelves.

The beautiful game

Mexico, Mexico, my father cried
as the blinding sun bubbled the paint from the window-sill
and his two thigh-waders flopped over
like drunk dogs on the back step
their sewage stink filling the room

from mending pipes fractured by car-bombs:
and everything was bully-beef before the telly
and every shout was, Shut your face!

as the sun beat down on the stadium waves:
Where is Mexico anyway? up past Templeton's Garage
the other side of the Sandy Row, a lamb chop on a plate

Emiliano Zapata, the Rio Grande, Geronimo
the soldiers crouched in the garden hedges
the policemen listening to radios in concrete sangars

the bruises on my face like big purple poppies
ankle plastered like an Alamo wound
from the gang who had caught me coming up the estate
as I left the only Protestant house on the Sierra Madre

fuck football: years later in Amsterdam
a friend took me to a back room in a seedy hotel
where I saw my first snuff movie

though I wasn't sure if it was real
a Mexican girl butchered on the bed of a filthy room
the bones pushed through the skin
cold and methodical, like my father shouting for England.

Consider my father eating an egg

If you were a reptile sleeping in the sun
immobile on a flat hot rock
face pock-marked with interconnected scales
lips closing over bead eyes
split tongue darting from between lips
skin flapping from neck and limbs

perhaps I would surprise you, cursed thing
smashing your thin head like an egg shell
send you to Dante's hell, lost soul without a soul
as you shimmy in the shadows of cacti
gravity-defying on an adobe wall
mindless as Catholic bells in a desert

but you react without thought
eyes scouting the room
salt-dispensing fingertips
before you attack
the soft-skinned egg in one quick gulp
into your roofless mouth

slipping down that sinewy throat
with every swallow of your Adam's apple
and is then gone
without satisfaction, the tongue-flick on a stupefied fly
or dead flies gathered in the glass bowl
of the overhead light
or water drawn into a flower's stem

and the look you give me as you catch me watching
like a man with yolk on his face
like a man who has just walked out of a desert
and found fragments of skull and bone
among the black sludge of a burning plane
that once was human
almost guilty on the end of a Lipton's spoon.

Peasants

Diego Rivera, what are you doing here?
not that we don't want you here,
but what are you doing here in the immensity of your Mexican colours

the slung girdles of poor priests' robes
the slung belt of cartridges
the swing of dull blooded scythes and bill hooks
the army of green maize shoots and kerchiefed Indian women
the great strides of giants in the foyer of the Rockefeller rich

like an old mission bell, what are you doing here Rivera
above this Ulster mantelpiece
in the gloom of a wet December Sunday?

See how the agent smokes his Embassy Red
his voice tapping in time to his plastic lighter on the armrest
I think I am going blind
like the rain on the window
like the grating of his militant voice.

And I know the old woman of this house is crazy
was married to an English soldier
booby-traps the entrances with brush-shafts –
she thinks we are Provos.

How I would like to sleep with Frida
in her big bed of exotic colours
with all the brown women of Mexico
in the scorching sun

but these people are real
know how to shoot guns
the proletariat are stuffed straw dolls for bayonet practice
are dust for gelignite
the smell of overcooked cabbage.

How big you are, Rivera
broader and taller than all the clean-cut heroic murals
big love words that silence even Neruda
that tears the tongues by the roots from all the priests
that frees us and Trotsky from this little man who wants to save us
wraps us up like dung smeared on adobe walls.

Shell

King Lear went mad listening to the sea
the rasping of cowrie shell-husks over one another
as the wind blew across them
like the squabbling of women's voices
dividing the kingdom of a hermit crab.

When he put spindle shells to his ear
he could hear the voices of the dead calling him,
not the sea.

And Caligula raided Britain
brought back open caskets of limpet,
razor, paddock, Pandora, tellin shells from his own shore –

but were they mad, or simply more perceptive?
like echoing voices in the huge coral caves
like a waiting Canute
a death-pale Annabel Lee?

Why does every adolescent girl decorate
her bedroom with shells
dream of sleeping sailors
or fishermen's huts dashed with shell
too old for the rough seas?

My father drove his supply lorry in '39
over a desert seabed millions of years old
the shells popping loudly under the wheels
like thousands of champagne corks
like rifles fired into soft bodies.

Oh listen to me! King Lear cried
I hear the sound of breaking bone
no lover lies beneath the creaking timbers of this house,
he gathers the whelk shells around his pallet of straw
to hear the murderer coming.

And they say that lovers who leap off Beachy Head
leave their last whisperings coiled
in the spiral hearts of shells forever,
that the sea itself is soundless.

Nina

I see your father among the cabbage patches
now that he is old he has become an imbecile
hoeing the ground, wearing a broken straw summer hat

he fears his mind is running away like Canada,
his sister died thinking of Canada

Canada is a large blank map on their bedroom wall
Canada is an airman's uniform at the table –

the fool, he should have stayed among his aerodynamic books,
he thought he knew you
I thought I knew you.

Nina, do you still have the twisted straw fertility dolls
you bought in an Indian village in Oaxaca
like thin money in a displaced Nigerian's pocket-book
like decadence in an East German's blue eyes
the dead eyes of straw dolls and Indians
and the men who lie broken-minded on your divan?

Persian flower, mouth, mother
John is dying from end-stage multiple sclerosis
you have known him for a long time
and fuck him though he is crying:

they are sending them to die now in square boxes
down in Switzerland with pills and plastic cups and digital
television
out beside a busy road and industrial estate
like slaughter houses for swine –

when I was a boy Sunday was a sin of waste
counting the Blue Circle Cement trucks
as they passed the high level-crossing like blurred clouds
and I knew then that the mind was big enough
to contain the randomness of the universe

but nothing is real in Berlin my love
the film companies have moved it to Prague or Krakow
like the emptiness in your suburban Berlin garden
in this middle-aged body these handicapped men
pay for with their pocket-money
in your father's memory-box
as he tries to remember what he is doing there.

I am sick of Berlin, the tired old sex-worker
I want to give everything back to the luggage-locker
the bicycle-clips, petrol bombs, leg callipers,
counting-cards, truss, condoms –
I want to tidy my mind like a morning room with a little sun.

South of the border

It is always the same, as though the film was freeze-framed
the black and white Saturday-night Western
the single-gauge track of iron rail made of twisted wallpaper
laid across the kitchen table between cake-box towns

the shantytowns of tents and swinging oil lamps
the unshaven men in vests and dirty hats
the washing-lines and stacks of wooden sleepers
the buffalo hunter and the poor silent Chinese coolies

all before the switch-off and the catechisms
for a drab unreal Sunday-school morning

but my heart went farther south across the border
wading the Rio Grande with the fugitives
the tall cacti and the colourful cantinas
where even the Apaches on the run were apathetic

and there is always a tall chapel-tower for snipers
and men in European cavalry striped pantaloons and big wide hats
and heroes who drank tequila not stout
and always blazing sun and thin long-horned cattle
and they all spoke English, but with a peculiar foreign accent

where you never heard the dull tight-lipped shouts
of the taciturn farmers at the Wednesday market.

And these heroes never used booby-trap bombs
under cars, or milk-churns, or in hedgerows, beneath dead lambs
Señoritas never sat all night by the radio
buckets of water and wet blankets under the windows

or sought the fool's gold of a far off country
and children never dreamed of jungle creepers and crashed biplanes
of Aztec temple ruins in a deeper Mexico.

Coatlicue

These men walk on water Nina
laughing above the spume, the silver glowing shoals
the passionsspiel in their German homes

bed-sits, flats, care-centres,
they lift themselves off old nails and answer the door.

You are their Goddess from Berlin, Coatlicue
ripping out hearts
lopped-off heads rolling down temple steps
blood to feed the rotting fields.

Teach them to breathe, masquerader
burn candles, undress.

Your second-hand car fleeting down the autobahn
in sub-zero temperatures
leaving behind the coffee drags, the mango skins
the broken plastic chairs in the communal garden
where the residents let their dogs shit.

These sad people in the sticks, beside the smelly Spree
will talk in hushed voices, in side rooms
about their dependents' need to communicate

to feel like living things:
these men are broken
but your middle-aged voluptuous body
topless with a skirt of snakes
will make them rise again.

Oh Coatlicue, see them now
no longer the limbless, the disfigured, the brain-damaged
sacrificing their false limbs, incontinence pants
their syndromes, neurological mis-wirings, birth de-sponses
for eighty Euros and masturbation.

Sand coloured cubes

Ricardo Legorreta is dead now
like a cinema reel that stops
or a curtain that is lifted on the blazing sun

and blinds us for a moment
in the whitewashed houses indifferent to revolution
the hand thrown bomb
the weedy schoolteacher with his manifesto
his Wall's ice-cream

the old men on the park benches
watching the lovers in the bushes
the Indians throw bricks at the ducks.

The Ulster indigenismo
the two faced God on Boa Island
stained in sacrificed blood
making histories from nothing

the Mayan and Aztec temples of new hotels
of glass and concrete and girders.

To kill a bird we paint it first
in orange or green
to kill a man we blindfold him
with newspapers and poverty and religion

to make a God we give him hands big enough to build
to drain river beds
pull up jungles
a voice in the doorway demanding two bob
for fortified wine.

Ricardo Legorreta is dead now
taking with him all that is exotic and cold
the modern myth
the jumbled brain that is dust

the auctioneer's shouts in a hillside farm
the five-pound paintings that are…

…five-pound paintings
the traction engines, the Massey Fergusons
the big English girl up in the rushes
the sand coloured cubes of the mind
that might or might not have been.

Wave

Geoffrey Firmin is at my booze again
he is standing out in the garden, in the rain
his suit is wet through, it is only morning
I don't think he knows it is raining hard
obscuring the glass, breaking the light
flooding the Ramblas into a torrent again

in my imagination: I am finding bottles
cheap brandy under the bed-linen in the airing-cupboard
and there is fresh blood in the vomit in the sink –
She is drinking again Geoffrey, he shrugs,
It's what we do, like the wino in the Barrigotic
he doesn't even try to beg, his naked torso
scorched in the sun, the skin of his back and arms

hanging loose, We all carry a map of the world
on our shoulders, she sighs, The Spanish are cruel, ask Lorca.
Where are you now? Has Geoffrey seen you?
No, he muses, looking among the dripping bushes
chasing cats. Do you feel alone? he asks,
She'll be back, when she's had enough
of the El Raval bars, and filthy beds.

Yes, we are all alone, like the cable-cars
swinging in the rain on the wire to the Castell de Montjuic
the sad and dangerous cannon in the Spanish Civil War museum
the drunk girl singing to the juke-box, and me waiting
pretending to work on poems, as Columbus
gazes out to sea and a new world that isn't new
and Geoffrey totters in the mud, turns and smiles, waving.

Yage

Before Howl there was Mexico, before Mexico
there was the Pound –
and we would take everything
prescription drugs, hash hashed with sweepings
and peat

and JoJo said, use the people against the Brits
as we slept in rooms with high white ceilings
sweating on Yage and Mexican guitars.

I knew Burroughs, the soft hat, the thin face
we had one at the corner of every terraced street
every patch of waste ground, outside the factories and the shipyard
pushing bennies and shit

as the Indian whores lined up along Corporation Street
brown skin under hard cold skies:
we had to get out, see ourselves from afar –

some old faggot with plucked eyebrows
in a Shell Suit, in the Bois de Boulogne
who asked if I smoked?

Madness ran in our family too, Allen
was more tolerated than sexuality
relations went 'for a rest'
came back convulsive-crazy with staring eyes
and bald patches
speaking in whispered riddles –

that was when they weren't shooting each other
or putting together bombs from toy chemistry sets
even our murals lacked colour or sand lizards
our shibboleths without blazing sun.

JoJo is dead, killed by his own egomaniacal-filled condom
Ginsberg is dead, Burroughs is dead
and I am sitting out my time in a builder's yard
in a Mexico of my own making.